ENGLISH BOOK ILLUSTRATION

THIS IS THE PICTURE OF THE OLD
HOUSE BY THE THAMES TO WHICH
THE PEOPLE OF THIS STORY WENT.
HEREAFTER FOLLOWS THE BOOK IT-
SELF WHICH IS CALLED NEWS FROM
NOWHERE OR AN EPOCH OF REST &
IS WRITTEN BY WILLIAM MORRIS.

C. M. GERE. Kelmscott Manor.
From *News from Nowhere* by W. Morris. 1891

ENGLISH
BOOK ILLUSTRATION

1800 - 1900

By

PHILIP JAMES

The KING PENGUIN *Books*
LONDON *and* NEW YORK
1947

THE KING PENGUIN BOOKS

Editor : N. B. L. Pevsner
Technical Editor : R. B. Fishenden

MADE IN GREAT BRITAIN

Text pages printed by EDMUND EVANS, LTD., LONDON
Collogravure plates by HARRISON & SONS, LTD., LONDON
Colour plates made and printed by JOHN SWAIN & SONS, LTD.,
who also made the line-blocks which appear in the text
Cover design by WILLIAM GRIMMOND

PUBLISHED BY

PENGUIN BOOKS, LTD.   PENGUIN BOOKS, INC.
HARMONDSWORTH, MIDDLESEX   245 FIFTH AVENUE
ENGLAND   NEW YORK

INTRODUCTION

A WORK on illustrated books, if it is itself to be illustrated, suffers one serious disadvantage. The original graphic processes—etching, wood-engraving, lithography and the rest—must inevitably lose some of their individual quality owing to the effect of photographic reproduction. Thus, a woodcut has to be reproduced by means of a line-block, an etching by photogravure, or an aquatint by photo-lithography. Again, illustrations of widely varying sizes must be made to conform with the format of the book in which they are reproduced. In this instance, therefore, it has been thought preferable to choose illustrations which require the minimum of reduction rather than to reproduce in little within the modest dimensions of this book some of the pages from larger books which readers would doubtless expect to find represented.

I am most grateful to those who have lent books from which reproductions have been made—Miss Helen MacGregor, Mr. R. B. Fishenden, Sir Harold Hartley, Sir Robert Leighton, Charles Prentice, Mrs. John Simmons and Mr. Iolo Williams. My thanks are also due to Mr. C. Harcourt Perry, who has re-engraved the Bewick feather.

The Director of the Victoria and Albert Museum kindly gave permission for a number of photographs to be made from books in the Museum Library, and Mr. C. B. Stevenson of the Laing Art Gallery, Newcastle-upon-Tyne, gave facilities for photographing the illustration by John Martin. Permission to reproduce has kindly been granted by Mrs. Pissarro for the illustration from "Christabel." Mrs. Sturge Moore lent the actual block engraved by her husband for de Guérin's *Bacchante*; and the Cambridge University Press lent the block for Richard Austin's vignette. Permission to reproduce illustrations has kindly been given by Messrs. Longmans Green & Co. (plate 13, page 30), Messrs. Macmillan & Co. (pages 44, 45, 52, 63), Messrs. Methuen & Co. (page 48), Sir William Nicholson (plate 14), the Proprietors of Punch (page 65), Messrs. George Routledge & Sons (pages 43, 33, 36, 37, 38, 39, 40, 50, plate 16), Messrs. Frederick Warne & Co. (pages 31, 42).

Finally, I must thank the Arts Council of Great Britain for permission to reproduce the technical notes which formed part of the introduction to the catalogue of the exhibition *English Illustrated Books* held at the National Gallery and in various provincial galleries.

PHILIP JAMES

R. AUSTIN. From Dodsley's *The Economy of Human Life.* 1808

ENGLISH BOOK ILLUSTRATION

1800-1900

Illustration and Decoration

AN illustrated book is a partnership between author and artist to which the artist contributes something which is a pictorial comment on the author's words or an interpretation of his meaning in another medium. This partnership works in a number of different ways. In a few rare instances the author and the artist are identified in a single person who himself carries out the designs. This union, as in the case of Blake, can result in a masterpiece comparable with the great achievements of creative art. But usually the illustration is the work of another hand, ideally a hand which itself carries out the design in whatever medium has been chosen. It is necessary to make this qualification because throughout the history of illustration there have been artists who have failed to assimilate one of the several techniques of graphic art which are suitable to take their place with printer's type. Then the artist has no control over the method chosen to reproduce his drawing and he must depend on the skill of the copyist. If the copyist is an artist of sensibility and a master of his medium he can produce an illustration of charm and quality; if he is merely a professional hack he can deaden and falsify the original design when he transfers it to the printing surface of wood, metal or stone. With the introduction of mechanical photographic processes towards the end of the nineteenth century the work of the living copyist was eliminated, and publishers, intoxicated with the power of the camera to give more or less exact representation of the original, were content to disregard the essential quality of illustration, namely, its power to blend with the rest of the book. Illustration is like décor in the ballet, one of several arts planned by a team of artists. Dance, drama, music and design together make a spectacle in which each has its share. Similarly, type, paper, binding and illustrations must all contribute to the art of the book.

While we are chiefly concerned with the illustration of imaginative literature, there are many books—perhaps they should be called books with illustrations rather than illustrated books—which cannot be altogether overlooked, especially in any survey of British illustration, for they are a characteristic product of the Englishman's traditional respect for the appearance of a book, whatever its subject may be. So there have been many scientific textbooks, trade catalogues or works on natural history, travel, art and archæology in which the illustrations are primarily a factual extension of the text, but which at the same time are a source of æsthetic pleasure. For instance, Audubon's princely elephant folio on the *Birds of America*, the unashamedly romantic *Temple of Flora* and a score of lesser natural history books, Ruskin's *Seven Lamps of Architecture* and *Modern Painters*, the catalogue of Sir Henry Thompson's blue and white porcelain illustrated by Whistler, or—when we come to modern technical illustration based on photography—a series such as the Shell Guides. All these have information as their chief aim, but are lovely and exciting to look at.

In the literary arts of poetry, prose and fiction the illustrator no longer aims at mere dispassionate visual description. In poetry, illustration is often altogether redundant. The lyric, concise in expression and compact in form, stands complete in itself. No distraction is tolerable. In narrative prose and fiction, however, the artist has a wide choice of pictorial incidents and descriptive scenes which, enlivened with a pictorial commentary which suggests another train of thought, he can interpret in images of his own choice. Successful interpretation implies the need for a reflection of the author's style. This may

8

seem a severe test, but it is one which all the real illustrators come through. To take a few examples. The etchings of Cruikshank are in perfect harmony with the literary idiom of Dickens; Millais and Trollope match each other in an exquisite unity; Lewis Carroll's combination of sheer nonsense and sober story-telling is reflected in Tenniel's drollery which has the air of reality; and Arthur Hughes and Christina Rossetti blend in the quintessence of Victorian sentiment, sweet but not cloying. All these partnerships were formed in the nineteenth century and all of them were the fusion of two contemporary minds in books which were often unpretentious, friendly pocket octavos with modest little woodcuts or shimmering silvery steel engravings. To-day, however, there is no longer that marked identity of aim between authors and illustrators. Our artists lean to a more stylised idiom which has little of the old vivid evocative quality, and taking advantage of the many recent technical developments in printing and colour-work they give us decoration rather than illustration. Illustrated fiction, once a source of rivalry between all the great publishing houses and the illustrator's main occupation, has now given way to screen fiction loaded with all the overtones of photographic naturalism. There is a tendency, therefore, to choose familiar texts on which the publisher and the professional typographer will build a book in which pride of place is given to the illustrations. The use of the finest craftsmanship and the best materials in all its parts makes for a large format more suited to the lap than the pocket, and so it becomes a picture book to be looked at rather than read. But picture books have a long and fine ancestry. There were the richly illuminated missals and breviaries for lords and abbots; noble library quartos with engraved plates supporting the elegant types of Caslon and Baskerville for country gentlemen of the eighteenth century; the annuals of the eighteen-thirties with their fashionable steel engravings; the table-books of the mid-Victorians bright with chromo-lithographs, and the self-conscious volumes from the private presses of the arts and

9

crafts movement. And now in the present generation, when machine-printing is no longer synonymous with bad taste but has been openly accepted and given its own style, the same standard is maintained in books such as *Urne Buriall* with Paul Nash's drawings done in colour-stencilled collotype, or *The Ancient Mariner* freshly interpreted through the exquisite fantasy of David Jones's line-engravings, or McKnight Kauffer's stylised commentary on that stylised classic *The Anatomy of Melancholy*, or—to mention the masterpieces of two of our best illustrators who lost their lives in the war—Rex Whistler's *Gulliver's Travels* and the Nonesuch Press edition of White's *History of Selborne* illustrated by Eric Ravilious.

All of these are picture books and they are all essentially in the English tradition.

Wood-engraving by L. CLENNEL after T. STOTHARD.
From *Pleasures of Memory* by S. Rogers. 1812

The English Tradition

WE have always had a native talent for book-illustration. Long before printing was invented manuscripts were adorned with superlative skill and great artistry by monkish craftsmen who ground their own colours, cut their own quills and pared the vellum pages in a lifelong labour of love which is far removed from the speed and precision of modern photographic processes giving thousands of faultless copies multiplied in a single hour by electrically driven machines. These early examples of the illustrator's skill, from the purely geometric complexities of the Celtic school in the time of the Venerable Bede to the earthy humorous naturalism of late Gothic work, are among the great glories of British art.

On the full pages of the Calendar where the traditional occupations of each month were depicted in initial letters, and among the tendrils and interlacings of marginal decoration, the whole pageant of English life was recorded. In the Luttrell Psalter, for instance, the smallest details of the East Anglian scene in the middle of the fourteenth century are set down. A travelling coach sets out filled with royal ladies one of whom receives a small dog from a horseman in attendance; a woman in a wimple plays with a squirrel; four men engage in pick-a-back wrestling; and a cripple seated in a wheelbarrow receives alms from a passer-by. The same intimacy, poetry and deep love of the country are found nearly five centuries later in Bewick's little woodcuts of the Northumbrian landscape. Boys build a snowman or chase a dog with a saucepan tied to its tail, or sit astride gravestones with wooden swords and make-believe soldiers' caps; pigs and hens rush through a gate carelessly left ajar by a retreating tramp and defile the dame's clean laundry which she is hanging out; the reaper, the poacher, the ferryman, the stonecracker each follows his humble calling. *Autres temps, autres mœurs*, but the same eye for homely details; the same instinctive knowledge of fur and feather; the same mystical apprehension of the seasons' changes, the elements, and the whole fabric of the countryside. Through a thousand years from Bede to Bewick our book-illustrators reveal that this intuitive awareness of nature is one of the dominant qualities of British art. In the nineteenth century it shines in all its strength in the two greatest painters of natural landscape who were the two greatest English painters of any kind, Turner and Constable. It is still the hallmark of our most serious and original artists. "The landscape painter must

walk in the fields with an humble mind," said Constable. This was exactly the belief of Constable's great contemporary in letters, the poet Wordsworth; and of all the illustrated books which might have been one can think of none more truly and essentially English than Wordsworth's poems illustrated by Constable. This would have united all the English qualities; the literary bias and the romantic flavour as well as the love of natural beauty.

The literary quality is an ingredient of our art which has far too often been belittled by the more severe critics. But literature in all its forms, notably poetry, has ever been the characteristic vehicle of the British genius, and the best of our painting is pervaded with the spirit of poetry. Rossetti, who combined the arts of painting and poetry in an unusual degree, wrote to Burne-Jones: "If any man has any poetry in him he should paint, for it has all been said and written, and they have scarcely begun to paint it". He and his fellow pre-Raphaelites carried over their painting of poetry into some remarkable illustrations, but just as the poetry of paint can sink to narrative prose, so a great number of the illustrations of the Victorian period degenerated into mere anecdotal story-telling, black and white versions of the popular history-paintings which men like Gilbert, Horsley, and Cope tossed off in such dreary profusion. A preoccupation with subject is naturally a characteristic of literary painting, and in the nineteenth century the subject was more often than not the romantic past, a past peopled by Dante, Arthur, Chaucer and other figures of chivalry whose world contrasted so strongly with the prevailing industrial ugliness.

If English art is literary it is also synonymous with romantic art. The literary impulse and the romantic temper have always gone hand in hand. They bred Shakespeare and Milton. In the eighteenth century the classical tradition gained for the time a strong foothold only to be followed by a romantic revival which swept aside its artificiality and the theories of selection, arrangement and generalisation, and brought a new feeling for the beauty of the natural world with an awakening to the picturesque, the sublime, the strange, the particular and the dramatic in nature. Artists toured the countryside in search of romantic views; at the same time they made portraits of the stately homes and parks of country gentlemen, and in passing they were not above giving a few painting lessons to the daughters of the house. They fed on the ruins of the Gothic monuments and exploited the prevalent architectural decay, interpreting it as the height of picturesque beauty.

The romantic illustration of this period is, therefore, to be found in all kinds of literary bypaths, in instruction-books for painters in water-colour, in essays on the theory of art, in guides for the amateur of conchology and botany, in fashion magazines, and in the innumerable topographical volumes which lured many an Englishman to Wales or to Scotland for the first time along metalled highways or, if he enjoyed an element of excitement and risk, on the new-fangled railways now spreading their tentacles through the length and breadth of the land. With the surge of industrial development that followed the railways, sheer stark ugliness prevailed everywhere, but at all times there were book artists who displayed a widely varying mixture of these three typical characteristics, the love of Nature, a literary bias and the romantic temper; and in so doing they maintained the English tradition.

T. BEWICK. From *The History of British Birds*

The Nineteenth Century

THE nineteenth century is in every way the most formative period in the history of book-illustration. It began with a revolution in all the arts. A new economic system was getting under way; a different social order was emerging; and startling developments in scientific knowledge altered the whole way of life. In the world of books this meant that publishers were looking for new methods which would produce cheaper books in larger editions and smaller formats with more illustrations. They availed themselves of various technical discoveries in other branches of graphic art, and during the first quarter of the century a remarkable range of processes was not only in use but was brought to a very high level of excellence.

Wood-engraving was rescued from its long eclipse in the shadow of line-engraving on copper only to be challenged immediately by the invention of lithography and steel-engraving. Mezzotint and aquatint with their emphasis on tonal rather than linear quality were favoured for the reproduction of works by the leading landscape artists, the former being a sympathetic medium for the reproduction of oil paintings in black and white, and the latter, with the addition of delicate hand-colouring, equally happy for the multiplication of the popular topographical subjects by the justly renowned English school of water-colourists. Next came the tremendous discovery of photography, an invention nearly as significant as printing itself and one which threatened the very existence of the illustrator. But in time every new technique is assimilated by the artist and the fluctuating struggle between the crafts and the machine becomes not a battle for extinction but a source of vitality. So in the incunabula of photographic illustration during the last two decades of the century we see artists already creating a new style in terms of the process or line-block. The camera holding a machine that harnessed light now replaced what had been a handicraft for five hundred years, and acid did in a few hours what the engraver had taken as many days to do. The camera was, of course, chiefly

WRITTEN TO BE SPOKEN BY

Mrs. SIDDONS.*

Yes, 'tis the pulse of life! my fears were vain!

I wake, I breathe, and am myself again.

* After a Tragedy, performed for her benefit, at the Theatre
Royal in Drury-lane, April 27, 1795.

Wood-engraving by L. CLENNEL after T. STOTHARD.
From *Pleasures of Memory* by S. Rogers. 1812

used for the mechanical facsimile reproduction of paintings and drawings first in monochrome and then in colour, but with this we have no concern here. The story of illustration in the nineteenth century is therefore inevitably bound up with the development and mastery of a great variety of technical methods which are described in greater detail in the notes following this introduction.

From a distance it is too easy to fix upon one year as a turning-point in history. The transition from one age to another is gradual if sometimes painful. So the year 1800 has no special virtue as a beginning, but it is a convenient landmark, and the concurrence of inventive genius and artistic skill at this date was indeed remarkable. During the latter part of the eighteenth century illustration had settled down to a level of rather dull competence. Line-engraving was the universal medium, the woodcut having long since been ousted by the copper-plate except for the crudities in chapbooks and ballad-sheets. Every literary classic was issued with plates and the contemporary fiction of Fielding, Smollett and Sterne was rich in incident for the engraver. In this field Thomas Stothard was the outstanding figure, and his greatest contribution lay in his designs for the numerous illustrated magazines now appearing, especially those in Harrison's *Novelists' Magazine*, It was of them that Lamb wrote:

> In my young days
> How often have I with a child's fond gaze
> Pored on the pictured wonders thou hadst done:
> Clarissa mournful, and prim Grandison!
> All Fielding's, Smollett's heroes rose to view;
> I saw and I believed the phantoms true.

Stothard lived on until 1834, working to the end. He found no difficulty in adapting his gentle, rather sweet classic style to the new manners and modes of the Regency, and in his microcosm we see the end of one great era and the beginning of another. (Plate 3 and illustrations on pages 10 and 15.)

T. BEWICK. From *The History of British Birds*. 1804

One has no difficulty in finding signs of new life in 1800. Bewick had rescued the woodcut from oblivion, and in his birds and animals, and above all in his vignettes (illustrations on pages 13, 17, 18, 19 and 20), he was laying the foundation of an English school of wood-engraving which continued throughout the century and is still unsurpassed. An obscure German artist named Senefelder had only three years earlier stumbled by chance on the lithographic process, which was to be one of the most fertile inventions in the history of illustration, especially when its use with colour had been mastered. Another German, the publisher Ackermann, had recently opened his famous Repository of the Arts in the Strand whence came innumerable volumes illustrated by the leading artists in aquatint and exquisitely coloured by hand. And, finally, William Blake was taking his "three years' slumber by the banks of Ocean" before starting on the last and greatest work in his unique series of Prophetic Books. In a single decade each of these four men made a highly individual contribution of major importance in the history of illustration.

Bewick was the first British wood-engraver to earn and

deserve a continental reputation. His greatness lies in the perfect harmony between his technique and his subject matter. Chief among his innovations was a new conception of the black and white picture. He did not think of it as a white space on which black outlines and solids made a linear design printed in relief, the background having been cut away to a lower level, as in the woodcuts of the fifteenth and sixteenth centuries, or in the crude illustrations in the chapbooks peddled round the country in the days of his youth. Instead he began with a black void out of which the subject appears in a varying range of grey tones with pure white for the lightest parts.

This creation of a grey tint gives the subject a "colour", an atmosphere, and a third-dimensional quality never before achieved in the woodcut. Type and illustration, too, are of equal weight. His figures are detached from their backgrounds and from the exquisite natural landscapes which abound in his vignettes, and all within a space the size of a florin. To attain this effect Bewick substituted the end-grain of a hard wood like box for the plank or side-grain of a softer fruit wood, attacked his block with a fine graver—it must be remembered that as an apprentice he

T. BEWICK. Vignette from *A History of British Birds*, Vol. II. 1804

T. Bewick. Vignette from *A History of Quadrupeds*. 1791

worked on a copper-plate—and lowered the height of those parts of the block which were to print a paler grey.

The dominating influence in Bewick's life was his love of the country and of country life. His intensity of feeling peeps out in his writings again and again. "I liked my master, I liked the business," he wrote of his apprentice days, "but to part from the country, and to leave all its beauties behind me, with which I had been all my life charmed in an extreme degree—and in a way I cannot describe—I can only say my heart was like to break." He may have felt inarticulate about nature but through his craft he became "a silent poet of the waysides and hedges", a poet who combined an astonishing accuracy of observation with sincerity, humour, occasionally a streak of healthy indelicacy, and not a little homely pathos. His art reaches its summit in his *General History of Quadrupeds* and *History of British Birds*. Here, in full-length portraits, the markings on a feather or the characteristic gait of every kind of animal from an elephant to a mouse are recorded with absolute fidelity. His beasts and birds all have their "very countenance and air" and each is set against an

T. BEWICK. The Cock. From *A History of British Birds*, Vol I. 1797

appropriate background; the cock in the farmyard, the woodcock in a leafy brake and the kingfisher by a stream. But it is the vignettes and tailpieces in these volumes that place Bewick among the great illustrators of all time. In them every feature of the countryside is lovingly recorded; its denizens, its implements, its aspect under rain, wind, sun and snow, and its trees and foliage in all seasons. They were the fruits of his daily walks to his father's colliery at Mickley Bank and to his school at Ovingham, and later of his visits to his home, always made on foot, from Newcastle twelve miles distant where he was apprenticed to the engraver Beilby in 1767.

By 1800 Bewick was in sole possession of the business. Associated with him were his younger brother John, who died in 1795, and a number of pupils most of whom, after contributing in varying degrees to their master's works, moved to London and developed an English school of engraving the influence of which lasted throughout the century. But even if they had the craftsmanship they did not have the vitality and originality of their master and they were unable to use the block as a vehicle for the direct transmission of a creative design by the artist himself. They attempted, as steel-engraving gained popularity in book-illustration, to imitate the effects of engraving on metal. So wood-engraving gradually sank to the level of a mere reproductive process and there it remained until it was eventually superseded as such by the half-tone block and at the same time was restored to its inevitable primacy as a medium for original creative decoration by William Morris.

Among Bewick's apprentices the more important were Anderson, Clennell, Harvey, Nesbit and Jackson. In time they all moved to London where there were only a few

W. HARVEY. The Jaguar. From *The Tower Managerie*. 1828

THE SNOW-DROP AND THE PRIMROSE.

Primrose ever sweet to view,
Beside a lovely Snow-drop grew;
They were the boasted pride of
      spring,   [wing;
Fann'd by the Zephy'rs balmy
Each thought itself the choicest flow'r
That ever drank the spangled show'r;
And vied for beauty, sought for praise,
Beneath the sun's resplendent rays.
At length the Snow-drop, fraught with ire,
Began to vent its jealous fire.

W. Harvey (engraved by D. Dodd). From Northcote's *Fables*. 1828

22

artists of any repute designing for or working on wood at this time. Harvey was the illustrator of several charming books, notably Northcote's *Fables* (illustrations on pages 21 and 22), and Clennell had ambitions as a painter—he was not unskilled as a water-colourist in a Cotmanesque style—and after cutting the designs of Stothard for Rogers' poems in a pleasing facsimile of the original pen-drawings, he abandoned illustrating for painting.

One other example of wood-engraving in the early years of the century must be mentioned, a splendid instance of the triumph of sheer genius over a quite rudimentary knowledge of the medium. This was Blake's solitary effort as a wood-engraver in Thornton's 1821 edition of Virgil's *Pastorals* (illustration on page 25). Thornton, a physician with a London practice and the publisher of several botanical works, including the famous *Temple of Flora* (Plate 10), deserves little credit for the inclusion of Blake's seventeen little jewels among the mediocrity of the remain-

W. Blake. From *Illustrations to the Book of Job*. 1826.

23

ing two hundred odd illustrations. It seems that we owe them to the persuasion of Linnell, Blake's friend and patron, who was also one of the doctor's patients, and a few other artists who could judge their real merit. Introduced with an apology from Thornton, wantonly trimmed by the printer and very unevenly printed, they none the less had an influence out of all proportion to their size. They were an inspiration to Blake's artist friends, above all to Samuel Palmer whose own perfect art owes so much to them. When one recalls the sepia drawings of Palmer's Shoreham period, or the prints of *The Bride* and *The Cyder Feast* by his friend Calvert, one must regret another opportunity lost by the publishers. Twenty-five years later Palmer did a few designs for Dickens's *Pictures from Italy*, and later still he contributed to three other books, but the deadening hand of the professional engraver robs these of Palmer's personal quality. Although he did not live to finish them, the etchings of his old age, when he too did designs for the *Eclogues* (Plate 7), justify his inclusion among the illustrators.

To return to Blake, it is his illuminated Prophetic Books which are an achievement unmatched in the history not merely of illustration but of all art. If his gifts are not expressed here with the technical mastery which he could show in the plates engraved for the publishers or in his own *Illustrations to the Book of Job* (see page 23), his visionary power appears in all its sublimity and its tenderness in this unique method of printing. Briefly stated, the process—a secret method, revealed in a dream, so Blake asserted, by his dead brother Robert—was etching in reverse. That is, the background was etched away with acid and the design was printed in relief in the same way as in a woodcut. Many of the copies were printed in colour applied by hand. Although the first illuminated books appeared in 1789 and several others before 1800 when Blake moved to Felpham, his two major and most impressive works in this medium, *Jerusalem* and *Milton*, were begun after his return to London. On *Jerusalem* he seems to have spent sixteen years, from 1804 to 1820; in the following

W. Blake. From *The Pastorals of Virgil.* 1821

year there came the Virgil wood-engravings, and in 1826, the year before his death, the line-engravings for the *Job* which are regarded by many as the climax of his career. The realisation of a theme which had possessed him for many years and the crystallisation of several essays in water-colour and pencil, they were at once the most original and the most technically direct and vital copper-engravings since the sixteenth century.

It was in 1823, the year in which Blake received his commission from Linnell for the *Job* engravings, that steel-engraving, borrowed from the printing of banknotes, was first used for book-illustration. The hardness of the metal permitted a virtually unlimited number of impressions to be taken from the plate, a fact which commended the new material to the publishers. It also gave a brilliance and luminosity which immediately attracted the great landscape artists Turner and Constable. Here was a medium which to some degree reproduced in black and white the feeling of air and light which they strove to capture in their paintings. Turner, who in the days of his apprenticeship had coloured mezzotints for J. Raphael Smith and had himself etched the outlines for his great series of mezzotints on copper, the *Liber Studiorum*, now did many drawings to be realised by the skilled professional engravers who served him so ably. The first volume was the set of plates issued in 1823 and known as *River Scenery in England*, but it was the vignettes in Rogers' *Poems* and the same poet's *Italy*, and those for Cadell's edition of Scott, that are Turner's great contribution to book-illustration proper (Plate 2). They almost seem to have been breathed on to the page; each subject melts away in an airy perspective on the dead white surface of the paper.

Turner was quite ready, too, to make a large number of sketches for conversion into steel-engravings for the many annuals, the *Keepsakes*, *Amulets*, *Literary Souvenirs*, *Forget-me-Nots* and the rest, which were now so popular. He was encouraged to do this by the financial rewards which were forthcoming—twenty-five guineas would be a normal sum for a trifling sketch—and by the realisation that an artist could speak through the cheap print to a vast public, a motive which also appealed to Constable who now secured the services of David Lucas to engrave a series of his landscapes. But left to themselves the steel-engravers, like the wood-engravers who followed Bewick, were unable to maintain a standard. They became mere professional copyists without any regard for the quality of the original picture, mere mechanical instruments without any outlet for individual expression. The process never recovered its vitality and was but little used again. If an artist wanted original work on metal he turned to etching direct on the plate, the art of Rembrandt or, in the period under review, of Cotman and then of Cruikshank, Palmer, Keene, Millais and, above all, of Whistler (Plate 8). Notable for working direct on steel in mezzotint, rather than employing the professionals, was the notorious John Martin, who as a painter aimed at what Lamb called "the material sublime". He achieved some remarkable illustrations to *Paradise Lost* and to the *Bible* (Plate 6) which, with their vast perspectives and fantastic architectural compositions, have a theatrical dream-like quality which anticipated the lithographs of Odilon Redon and the other pioneer surrealists.

Just as steel-engraving was appreciated for its commercial value, so the new art of lithography was first used for its reproductive rather than its æsthetic qualities. Although it was brought to this country by Senefelder's agent in 1800 and inspired a group of artists, including Blake, Stothard and Fuseli, to make some trial proofs which were issued in 1803 under the forbidding title of *Specimens of Polyautography*, it was not until the'twenties that it became established as a method of book-illustration. It soon competed with engraving in the printing of music and, being a process completely in accord with the romantic mood of the moment, it commended itself to the amateur artists who flocked to the Continent with their sketch-books at the close of the European war and returned with a few results worthy of circulation among friends. A number of instruction books with plates and diagrams by David Cox and other quite eminent artists were also issued for the encouragement of these amateurs. The successive stages of a drawing, whether in pen, pencil or brushwork, could be admirably reproduced by lithography which could give every kind of effect. No one intervened between the artist and the illustration, which appeared exactly as drawn. But it was not until an English version of Senefelder's treatise on his discovery was published by Ackermann in 1819 that any substantial use was made of the new process. It then had a vogue in the reproduction of the large topographical drawings by Roberts, Haghe and Prout, who were prolific in their recordings of mediæval architecture in the Low Countries and Germany, or of town and country life and customs in France and Italy. A rather more original use of lithography was made by John Doyle, father of the better-known "Dicky" Doyle, in his political caricatures, and it was used for the reproduction of the original edition of Edward Lear's immortal *Book of Nonsense* which appeared in 1846; but there was nothing in this country to compare with the magnificent virtuosity of Daumier or Gavarni who were creating a truly democratic art in this medium.

The only English artist who could have rivalled the French lithographers was Rowlandson. He, too, was a born illustrator but he chose the aquatint as his means of expression. It would perhaps be nearer the truth to say that the versatile and ingenious Mr. Ackermann chose it for him as he was continuously employed by this publisher and doubtless counted for his bread and butter on the work in the numerous volumes of topography and social comedy which came from the Repository in the Strand. He was at his best, as always, in his figure-drawings for the *Microcosm of London*, the *English Dance of Death* (Plate 9), and the various *Tours of Doctor Syntax* which achieved an astonishing popularity in spite of the trite pedantry of the verses. His versatility was great. In his conversation pieces of paunchy aldermen and spindly rakes there is a brutal realism, and in his pastoral scenes a surprising and quite moving tenderness and delicacy.

The English aquatint was a characteristic and unique contribution to illustration, and although it had been popularised if not introduced by Paul Sandby, the so-called father of English water-colour, it was only Ackermann who exploited it with such good taste. The actual drawing of the composition would be done by the artist himself, who then handed it over to the team of professional colourists, many of them children, and a number of French emigrés, who showed a marked degree of sensibility in their share of the work. Such a technique was admirably suited for the reproduction of water-colour in topographical volumes, and it was also used with great effect to illustrate the high life of the Regency bucks and blades, typified by Jerry Hawthorn in Pierce Egan's *Life in London,* which was a subject for Cruikshank's caustic wit.

In this and other of his early works Cruikshank used aquatint, but he soon chose etching as his medium, a technique which with its fluent line was commonly used by our humorous and satirical draughtsmen. His output was prodigious. Hundreds of his drawings were also engraved on wood; but it is by his own etchings for the fairy tales by the brothers Grimm, for Dickens and for the *Comic Almanack* that he will always be remembered. For a sustained effort, even by one to whom drawing came as naturally as talk, the *Comic Almanack* is unsurpassed, and as a visual record of London life in the first years of Victoria's reign it is a fascinating document (Plate 5). At the same time he was working in his short-lived partnership with Dickens, and here we can measure his real greatness. His illustrations to *Oliver Twist* or the *Memoirs of Joseph Grimaldi* make those by "Phiz", the commonly acknowledged illustrator of Dickens, seem tame in conception and feeble in drawing (Plate 4). Cruikshank etched as Dickens wrote. Both were townsmen to the core and cockneys to their finger-tips. London, with its fog, its flickering gaslight, its shabby courtyards, its waterside, its gaiety and its squalor, leaps to life through

R. Doyle. Hyghest Court of Law in ye Kingdom. Ye Lords hearing

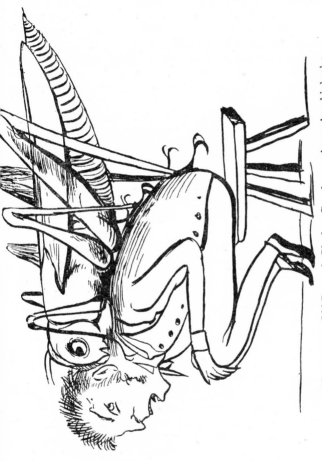

There was an Old Person in Black, a Grasshopper jumped on his back ;
When it chirped in his ear, he was smitten with fear,
That helpless Old Person in Black.

E. LEAR. *More Nonsense.* 1872

their art. Both were fascinated by the grotesque in man and nature, by twisted minds and distorted bodies. Both were crusaders for social reform and attacked with equal pungency of word and line the cruelty of the charity schools and workhouses, and the drunkenness and vice which became rampant with the new industrial era. Cruikshank stands midway in the long line of humorous and satirical draughtsmen from Hogarth onwards who, through their illustrations and prints, have provided an important chapter in the history of English art.

Cruikshank's contemporaries, John Leech (Plate 11), "Dicky" Doyle and Keene (illustrations on pages 30 and 34), were of a different kidney. Less splenetic, more humorous, they laughed with and at the prosperous new middle classes. They joked about their efforts to adjust themselves to a life full of excitement and sprinkled with amusing mishaps. Railways were changing the face of England; steamboats, the electric telegraph and the penny post had increased the tempo of living to an unprecedented speed. All this was reflected in books and especially in magazines. The demand for cheap illustrated literature had produced Knight's *Penny Magazine* in 1832, and illustrations of every interesting event at home and abroad were expected by a population now becoming news conscious. In 1841 *Punch* appeared; in the following year *The Illustrated London News*. In 1848 an enterprising businessman named W. H. Smith started railway bookstalls. It was the roaring 'forties.

This feverish activity was marked by a deplorable decline in the standard of craftsmanship. Wood-engraving was debauched by the new journalism and deadened by the professional hacks who interpreted the slender talent of the historical and landscape painters Stanfield, Birket Foster, Gilbert (illustration on page 33), and the rest. No one who knows the original drawings made by Leech and Keene for the young *Punch* can fail to see how they were vulgarised in the cutting. And yet even in these middle years of the century, the dark age of illustration and of all the arts, the book was the one material object so strongly supported

SIR J. GILBERT. Lear fantastically dressed with flowers. From Staunton's *Shakespeare's Works*. 1856-58

C. Keene. From *Mrs. Caudle's Curtain Lectures*. By D. Jerrold. 1866

by a tradition of good taste that it was not completely debased by the genius for ugliness displayed in our grandparents' buildings and household goods.

It was in coloured illustration that the mid-Victorians made their most effective contribution. Much of it was solid, exuberant and tasteless. Some of it, when the printer happened to be a man of sensibility, was most pleasing. Hitherto the colour had been applied by hand and illustrators had taken their cue from the print-makers. The coloured mezzotints which so agreeably depicted town and country life in the reign of George III and the aquatint views of Ackermann's period had also served a purpose apart from book-illustration. They were the ancestors of the modern photographic colour reproductions which the fine arts trade still supplies to thousands of homes, for they were often reproductions of popular pictures made for those who could not afford originals. Now again a colour-printer provided a new technique which was absorbed by publishers for the purposes of illustration. This was the colour process invented in 1835 by George Baxter of Lewes. Baxter worked in oil colours from a large number of wood-blocks, sometimes as many as twenty, with a remarkable precision of register. He first attempted some dingy unsuccessful book-illustrations, but his real aim was picture-printing in imitation of oil painting. He was a born populariser, a self-appointed missionary with the task of spreading taste through colour-printing. His determination to combine technical perfection with popular prices brought him to bankruptcy, but others carried on his process by licence and used it extensively for illustration. In particular he pointed the way to a method of colour-illustration from wood blocks which was developed by a skilled and sensitive craftsman named Edmund Evans. Evans will always be remembered as the printer in Racquet Court who gave to English children their nursery classics by Walter Crane, Caldecott and Kate Greenaway.

The decline in black and white art in the middle of the century was succeeded by a sudden flowering, which began with a few remarkable books from 1855 onwards and lasted until 1875. This revival, often acclaimed as the heyday of British illustration, must however be viewed with a due sense of proportion. No period has been so extravagantly praised or so thoroughly documented. Undeniably there was a galaxy of talent both among the artists who drew the designs and the engravers who cut the blocks. In fact, it was this conjunction of inspiration and craftsmanship which

D. G. Rossetti. *The Maids of Elfen-Mere.* By W. Allingham.
1855

D. G. ROSSETTI. St. Cecilia. From Tennyson's *Poems*. 1857

gave the movement such vitality. But the divorce between mind and hand persisted, and however skilled the professional copyists might be—and no one would question the amazing virtuosity of the Dalziel Brothers, Swain, Linton and others—there could never exist that unity which Bewick gave to his books in which he, as the originator of the designs himself, cut the blocks and supervised the press work. Illustrated books were now quite unrelated in their

Sir J. E. Millais. Edward Gray. From Tennyson's *Poems*. 1857

parts. Individual illustrations were good, but publishers and editors were capricious in their choice and mixture of artists in one volume, and they showed a deplorable taste in all the other ingredients of book-building. A lack of confidence, which sometimes grew into open enmity, existed between the artist and the engraver. William Allingham, whose book of poems issued in 1855 was the first landmark of the movement, speaks of his illustrators as "those excellent painters who on my behalf have submitted their genius to the risks of wood-engraving". Here he refers to Rossetti, Millais and Hughes, whom he aptly

Sir J. E. Millais. The Hidden Treasure. From *Parables of Our Lord.* 1864

G. J. PINWELL. The Goose. From *Wayside Posies*. 1867

describes as painters, for it was Rossetti's refusal to lay aside the tones of paint and understand the limitations of the wood block that led to his early withdrawal. He wrote of his design for *The Maids of Elfen-mere* (illustration on page 36) in Allingham's poems that it "used to be by me until it became the exclusive work of Dalziel, who cut it!" The Dalziels retorted with some justice that Rossetti "made use of wash, pencil, coloured chalk and pen and ink". In spite of these difficulties the Pre-Raphaelites and their immediate associates, gifted with a youthful ardour and a fresh intensity of vision, stand far above the general run of illustrators—how far may be seen in the next important book, the famous Tennyson published by Moxon in 1857

W. MULREADY. From Goldsmith's *The Vicar of Wakefield*. 1843

(illustrations on pages 37 and 38), which includes a number of the old stagers from the preceding generation, such as Mulready (illustration below) and Maclise.

In addition to Rossetti, Millais and Holman Hunt who were members of the Pre-Raphaelite brotherhood, the best illustrators of the 'sixties were Hughes, Sandys, Pinwell, Keene, Walker, North, Tenniel and Houghton (illustration below). There were many other able performers, and some indication of the great output is found in the list of more

SANCHO AND
HIS DAPPLE

A. Boyd Houghton. From *Don Quixote*. 1866

A. Hughes. From *Sing-Song* by C. Rossetti. 1872

important books compiled by Forrest Reid in his exhaustive survey of the period. He gives over four hundred titles covering some sixty artists, and this does not include the numerous magazines such as *Once a Week* and *Good Words* in which much of their best work appeared. Generally it is the books illustrated by a single artist rather than the volumes with a hotch-potch of illustrators which are the most satisfactory. One thinks at once of Millais's masterpiece, *The Parables of Our Lord* (illustration on page 39); *Mrs. Caudle's Curtain Lectures* (illustration on page 34), one of the comparatively few books illustrated by that superb draughtsman Keene; Christina Rossetti's *Sing Song* (illustration above), or Macdonald's *At the Back of the North Wind* by which Hughes will always be remembered; and, of course, the two *Alices* where Tenniel, stimulated by the criticism of Carroll, excelled all his previous and subsequent efforts

L. CARROLL. From a facsimile of the original manuscript of *Alice's Adventures Underground.* 1886. (For Tenniel's version, see facing page.)

44

(illustrations on pages 44 and 45). Two artists who, although they have no complete books to their credit, come near to the Pre-Raphaelites in skill and originality, are Sandys (illustration on page 46) and Pinwell (illustration on page 40). If they lacked some of the Pre-Raphaelite poetry, they showed a far greater understanding of their medium. An original drawing by Sandys differs very little from the wood-engraving and a design by Pinwell seems positively to gain in substance and intensity after it has been cut on the block.

It will be observed that many of the best illustrations of the period are in children's books; the English nursery was now most nobly served. The movement of the 'sixties expired as abruptly as it had begun, and in the period of stagnation which followed, the only vitality to be seen was in the children's books illustrated by Walter Crane,

F. SANDYS. Amor Mundi. From *The Shilling Magazine.* 1865

Randolph Caldecott (Plate 12), and Kate Greenaway, who were all presented through the charming colour-printing of Edmund Evans. There is an element of escapism which shows itself clearly in their individual and tasteful art, a foreshadowing of the open revolt against machine-art which was to come through a revival of craftsmanship and a return to earlier styles. Kate Greenaway, encouraged by laudatory letters from Ruskin, created a world of children charmingly clad in fancy-dress of no known period (Plate 16 and illustration on page 50). Caldecott withdrew to the rural England of the eighteenth century as it appeared in the poems of Cowper and Goldsmith which he illustrates. Crane, however, was a more important figure. He evolved a style which derived from his association with Morris and Burne-Jones and had a lasting influence on his young contemporaries. An active member of the Arts and Crafts Movement, he did not fall under the spell of its archaism but showed an individual decorative sense based on classical motives and was ready to design for the modern printed page rather than seek inspiration from mediæval manuscripts. His early toy-books such as *The Three Bears* or *Mother Hubbard*, depicting delightful interiors and graceful figures in richly patterned garments, are remarkably strong. Their solid areas of flat contrasted colours reflect the influence of Japanese prints which were now appearing in the Western world and enthralling its artists. One other book of this period illustrated in colour and again printed by Evans deserves to be mentioned. This was "Dicky" Doyle's set of charming drawings to William Allingham's poem *In Fairyland* (Plate 13). Here he discards his earlier style of thin outline and with the support of Evans at his best as a colour-printer he achieves a masterpiece.

The art of black and white provided a striking contrast. In 1875 three of the best artists who had worked through the 'sixties—Hughes, Pinwell and Houghton—all died in their prime. In the following year technical developments brought professional wood-engraving to abysmal depths. Photography also was nearing the end of its gestation and

Caput apri defero,
Reddens laudes Domino.
The boar's head in hand bring I,
With garlands gay and rosemary ;
I pray you all sing merrily,
       Qui estis in convivio.

The boar's head, I understand,
Is the chief service in this land ;
Look, wherever it be fand,
       Servite cum cantico.

W. CRANE. From *A Book of Christian Verse, selected* by H. C. Beeching.
1895

was now generally used as a method of transferring a design on to the wood block. As far back as 1835, while Baxter had been patenting his colour-process, Fox Talbot was taking his first paper "sun-pictures" at Lacock Abbey. Four years later he communicated his discoveries to the world, while Daguerre quite independently did the same in France. The invention was ridiculed in the Press and guyed by the caricaturists, but it was destined to change the whole basis of illustration in another fifty years. Fox Talbot published some of his studies in 1844 as a book which he called *The Pencil of Nature*, and a brief fashion for books illustrated with real photographs soon followed. But the first real intrusion of the camera into illustration was its occasional use to photograph the drawing on to a sensitised wood block. This had the effect of weakening the engraver's tyranny over the artist who had often been content to supply a sketch rather than a printed drawing which the master engraver would interpret rather than copy. In addition the artist's original could now be preserved, for hitherto it had been drawn direct on to a whitened block or, if on paper of the size of the block, had been cut to pieces. Now a drawing could be of any size provided it was of the correct proportions.

Other factors in the deterioration of engraving were the demand for bigger and yet bigger blocks by the illustrated journals and the introduction of the mechanical ruling of parallel lines which killed the art as earlier it had killed steel-engraving. Mechanical ruling permitted a vast increase of range in the tonal values so that artists gave up any attempt to design for the wood and merely sent wash drawings to the engraver. In America especially this style captured the publishers and public alike. But no artists of real merit exploited the possibilities of the new technique with the exception of Doré whose illustrations now had a great vogue. He was an artist of real power, often a forbidding power with which he made a moving indictment of social evils in his scenes of London; but he was a Frenchman and employed French engravers.

S s
T t
U u
V v
W w
X x

K. Greenaway. From W. F. Mavor's *The English Spelling Book.* 1885

The ten years between 1875 and 1885 have aptly been called "the no-man's land between woodcut and process"; and it was in this decade that the elimination of the human engraver by mechanical methods proceeded to its inevitable conclusion. Photography had already been applied experimentally to the three basic methods of illustration—relief, intaglio and surface-printing. This union resulted in the line-block and half-tone as relief processes, the photogravure as an intaglio or incised process, and photo-lithography and collotype as surface processes. The application of colour to all of these was only a matter of time, and soon photographic illustration had established itself as a cheap and quick method for the facsimile reproduction of drawings and paintings. The half-tone and the three-colour process with their screen technique and printing-surface of tiny dots required a coated clay paper for successful results. This unwelcome legacy we still inherit, but it was now hailed with delight by a public as yet unaware of the impressionists to whom photographic accuracy was the sole criterion of merit.

In the line-block, however, a new and satisfactory method of reproducing a drawing was found, provided that the artist accepted the limitations of clear black lines and masses and pure white spaces without any intermediate "half" tones. While the new technique was at first an economic rather than an æsthetic success, a new school of illustrators saw in it a satisfactory means of translating their pen-and-ink drawings. These so-called pen-draughtsmen, headed by Hugh Thomson and the Brocks, illustrated several rival series of standard novels by Jane Austen, Mrs. Gaskell, Maria Edgeworth and other authors where old-world scenes were recreated with an accurate representation of all the period accessories of architecture, costume and furniture. Much of their charm lies in the seeming fineness of line which make their vignettes harmonise so pleasantly with the printed page, but this is largely due to the ability of the camera to reduce their original drawings which were usually of a far greater size than the block. The

"In the most pathetic parts
of my sermon,"

H. Thomson. From Goldsmith's *The Vicar of Wakefield.* 1890

change-over from wood to line-block was rapid. It was in
the April 1886 issue of the *English Magazine* that Thomson's
drawings were first reproduced by the new method (illustration on page 52), and when we reach the 'nineties,
commercial wood-engraving is virtually dead.

The last decade of the century provides a truly remarkable conclusion to this brief survey. In it we see a constellation of artists which was dazzling even in comparison with the crowded 'sixties. And now there was a far greater profusion of talent, as prolific as it was varied, and a far more adventurous use of materials. In the technical field the line-block was established as a medium for creative work, the original woodcut was restored to its true position as a partner with print, and lithography and etching were revived as illustrative methods for the original artist.

Among the artists two strangely contrasted figures dominate the scene: William Morris and Aubrey Beardsley. The one was born out of his time; the other was very much a product of the *fin de siècle* with its deliberate cultivation of all that was artificial, perverse and mannered.

In 1890 Beardsley was only eighteen and an insurance clerk. In 1898 he died of tuberculosis in the France he loved whence came *Mademoiselle de Maupin* and *A Rebours* and the whole vocabulary of decadence by which he was haunted. In the intervening years, driven by that incredible intensity common to consumptives, he did over a thousand drawings, each for some definite purpose. He was a townsman and liked to work in a room hung with black velvet curtains and lighted by candles. He began like a good Pre-Raphaelite with illustrations to the *Morte d'Arthur* and was encouraged by Burne-Jones as much as he was discouraged by Morris who was affronted by his rococo treatment of the Arthurian legend.

The influence of the Pre-Raphaelites soon waned and gave way to the Japanese print, as his drawings for Oscar Wilde's *Salome* show. But this in time yielded to the illustrators of the eighteenth century, who inspired him to his greatest work—his design for Pope's *The Rape of the Lock* (illustrations on pages 54 and 55) and for his own erotic romance *Under the Hill*, which appeared in *The Savoy* magazine. In these he invents an entirely original technique in black and white and achieves a triumphant mastery over the limitations of the line-block as a reproductive medium.

A. BEARSDLEY. The Battle of Beaux and Belles.
From Pope's *The Rape of the Lock.* 1896

A. BEARDSLEY. The Baron's Prayer.
From Pope's *The Rape of the Lock.* 1896

The wonderful range of his greys and the brilliance and sparkle of his pure blacks and whites are reproduced without any loss by the way; and the dotted and patterned areas which he devised to represent the materials in which he clothed his figures gives a wonderful effectof richness and colour.

William Morris provides a striking contrast to Beardsley. Physically robust, always drawing on his love and knowledge of the English countryside and intolerant of the artificiality of urban culture, he concentrated his whole being in a heroic fight against the squalor of the industrial age. The effects of the machine and mass-production could only be countered by a return to the mediæval system of guilds. Convinced of the rightness of Ruskin's doctrine of "joy and work" and of his own duty to put this gospel into effect, he himself practised many crafts, running workshops at Merton Abbey for the goods which he and his associates made, and selling them in the famous shop in Oxford Street.

Printing was the last of his adventures and the foundation of the Kelmscott Press in Hammersmith was the crowning glory of his career. Here again he wished to make a practical and creative protest against the vulgarity and meanness of contemporary printing and once more he looked backwards to the earliest printers for a pattern. It is as a printer and book-designer rather than as an illustrator that he takes his place as a great master of typography. His insistence on good materials and fine proportions in all parts of the book was of far greater significance than his splendid antiquarian revival of borders, initials and type from famous incunabula (see frontispiece and page 57). But for all its unwieldy size and archaic decorations the noble folio *Chaucer*, with its illustrations by his lifelong friend Burne-Jones, will remain one of the great books of all time. The illustrations were cut on wood by a very able craftsman, W. H. Hooper, from drawings made by Catterson Smith after the originals of Burne-Jones. In spite of this double intervention the decorative romantic style with its elementary scheme of

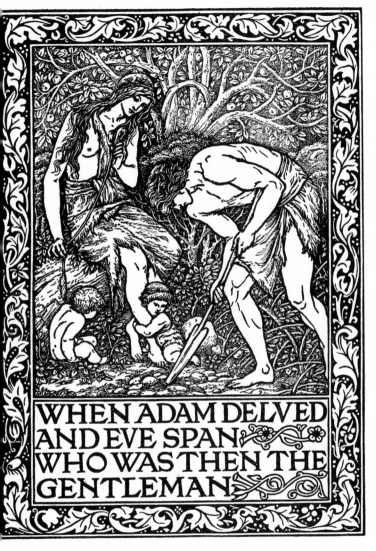

WHEN ADAM DELVED
AND EVE SPAN·
WHO WAS THEN THE
GENTLEMAN·

Sir E. Burne-Jones. From W. Morris's *A Dream of John Ball*. 1892

representation is ideal for the purpose. It gives the effect of a remote world, as far removed from everyday life as Morris's books were. The restoration of the woodcut as the natural partner of print was an essential part of Morris's plan, and he employed a number of designers, notably a group from the Birmingham School, including E. H. New, C. M. Gere (see frontispiece) and Arthur Gaskin. During the years 1891 to 1898 fifty-three books in all were issued. Morris just lived to see the *Chaucer* before he died in October 1896.

Second only to Morris in his reverence for craftsmanship but a greater immediate influence on artists and publishers was Charles Ricketts (illustration on page 59). Although he turned to the Renaissance, to Florentine idealism rather than to Morris's gothic naturalism, he adopted the more practical line of persuading commercial publishers to accept the standards of the select presses, and Oscar Wilde's *The Sphinx* which he designed and decorated and which John Lane published from the Bodley Head is perhaps the most remarkable book of the period. His own lovely volumes, notably the *Daphnis and Chloe*, the first book from the Vale Press which he and his friend and partner Shannon planned together in every detail, were less self-conscious than the Kelmscott books and had a far greater effect on general taste.

In Morris's typography one senses a complete organic growth with its roots in the arts and crafts of which he was a master: in Ricketts's, less urgency, a cool scholarly precision, a crystalline purity of form. By both the block is treated as a white rectangle with linear pattern and occasional spots of glowing black, in the manner of the fifteenth-century masters.

Two other artists, closely associated with Ricketts, did personal and memorable work. Lucien Pissarro, the son of Camille, had done some illustrations for the Vale Press before he started to issue his own books from the Eragny Press (Plate 15). He is less important than Ricketts if only because he was content to accept the unreal economy of

DAPHNIS IS SAVED FROM THE PIRATES BY
THE FORTUNATE PIPING OF CHLOE .

While he was muttering this passion, a Grashopper that fled
from a swallow, took Sanctuary in Chloes bosome, and the
pursuer could not take her; but her wing, by reason of her close
pursuit, slapt the girle upon the cheek; but she, not knowing what
was done, cryed out, and started from her sleep.   But when she
saw the swallow flying near by, and Daphnis laughing at her
17   fear,

C. RICKETTS.   From *Daphnis and Chloe* (Vale Press).   1893

59

the private press, but as one of the artist-craftsmen who was printer, type-designer and illustrator in one he achieved a simplicity and unity which give the Eragny books a special loveliness, above all those which he printed in colour. Sturge Moore had a close affinity with Ricketts (illustration on page 61); he too had a tremulous poetic line. But he attacked the block in the manner of Bewick, Blake and Calvert. To him it was not a white background for forms in outline but a black void out of which he bodied forth his demi-gods and centaurs. Some of his finest work was done for that remarkable magazine *The Dial*, which was Ricketts's first venture in book-production. This large, sumptuous quarto, which has some exquisite lithographs by Shannon, was one of the earliest of that crop of art periodicals which appeared through the 'nineties in numbers unheard of before or since. Throughout the century illustration had been influenced by the periodical press, which has always tempted publishers and artists alike with the financial rewards offered by a large and regular circulation. But now the motive was rather one of genuine determination on the part of subjective artists to publish contemporary work however daring in whatever medium might be chosen. As a result there was a succession of short-lived quarterlies and annuals most of which, unlike *The Dial*, lacked artistic unity owing to the wanton intrusion of half-tone reproductions of paintings and drawings. This is true of the notorious *Yellow Book* and *The Savoy*, both of which are now remembered chiefly for Beardsley's contributions. But in their pages we can also see the work of the English impressionists—Sickert, Steer, Rothenstein and Conder. *The Dome*, *The Quarto*, *The Pageant*, *The Venture* and Gordon Craig's very personal *The Page* were some of the more interesting of these ephemeral journals.

Apart from the creative work in these experimental magazines and the books of the private presses, together with the few commercial editions inspired by them, there was also a great output of less adventurous illustration. The line-block, having been used in its own right with great

T. Sturge Moore. From De Guérin, *The Centaur and The Bacchante.*
1890

originality by Beardsley, Sime, Housman (illustration on
page 62) and others, now became the usual reproductive
process for pen-and-ink drawings of the more traditional
kind. First there was Phil May (illustration on page 64),
who in the field of humorous drawing was a worthy suc-
cessor to Leech, Keene and Du Maurier and a draughtsman
more versatile than any of them. With wit and humour
he combined great simplicity and economy of line, and into
his sketches of guttersnipes and ragamuffins of all ages and
both sexes, which he depicted with such genius, he brought
a tragic realism recalling the weaknesses and misfortunes of
his own life. E. J. Sullivan was a skilful draughtsman with a
strong personal style, sometimes rather grim and sardonic.
His friend A. S. Hartick, still well known as a charming
and sensitive artist, Walter Crane and Anning Bell in the
decorative school, William Strang, primarily an etcher,
were only some of the black and white artists whose work
has not faded with the passage of time.

L. HOUSMAN. From C. Rossetti's *Goblin Market*. 1893

Professional wood-engraving had been killed by the camera and by its own virtuosity and now colour-work too was caught in the toils of the commercial reproductive processes. But, as the history of art has so often shown, those artists who struggle with the limitation of a new technique show results of the greatest sensitivity. So we find Rackham and Menpes, the former in his children's books with an essentially English treatment of a world half real and half fairy, and the latter in his Whistlerian colour sketches of the South African war, displaying a commendable restraint in the use of the three-colour process which was soon to be so shockingly vulgarised in the representation of a sickly and ever more highly coloured naturalism.

The British painters who accepted the impressionist doctrine seldom worked as illustrators in the manner of their French predecessors who did not hesitate to master the graphic arts and use the original processes in which the artist was in control of his design from the first sketch to its final appearance on the printed page. In William Nicholson, however, we see a painter who, after studying in Paris and coming under the influence notably of Toulouse-Lautrec, made a really original contribution to book illustration (Plate 14). His splendid series of quartos, of which *London Types*, *The Almanac of Twelve Sports* and *An Alphabet* are the most remarkable, will live. In style they recall, with their bold dark masses lighted with touches of subdued and lovely colour, the masterly posters which Nicholson and his brother-in-law James Pryde had brought out under the pseudonym of the Beggarstaff Brothers. They also owe not a little to the frankly imitative chapbooks decorated by Joseph Crawhall, who issued a charming series from Newcastle, one of the traditional homes of the chapbook. In subject they are racy in an English way and essentially of their time. In technique they mark the reinstatement of the original artist unhampered by the deadening hand of the hack engraver. Nicholson himself cut the blocks and coloured them by hand. The designs were actually lithographed for the ordinary editions, but

VANITAS. *Pantomime Child* (to admiring friend). "Yus, and there's another hadvantage in bein' a hactress. You get yer fortygraphs took for noffink!"   P. MAY. From *Punch*. 27th Nov. 1901

lithography of all the reproductive techniques used on a commercial scale permits the artist to present his design with the minimum of interference.

And it is on this theme, the need for integrity on the part of the publisher in reproducing the artist's work, that we may appropriately bring this short survey to an end. The tradition laid at the beginning of our period by Bewick, although almost completely obscured at times by the commercial standards of the industrial age, was reaffirmed with magisterial authority by William Morris as the century drew to its close.

The succeeding revival in the arts of the book and the general acceptance of the machine in our own time may have given us so far only the first fruits of a new art of illustration. Whatever may be in store we can always agree with Morris when he said that the illustrated book "is not, perhaps, absolutely necessary to man's life, but it gives us such endless pleasure, and is so intimately connected with the other absolutely necessary art of imaginative literature that it must remain one of the very worthiest things towards the production of which reasonable men should strive".

TECHNICAL NOTE

As the foregoing pages indicate, the nineteenth century was marked by a wide variety of illustrative processes. These ranged from crafts practised without change since the fifteenth century to the application of photography to printing. The progress of the latter, in our time, has been so rapid and is so closely bound up with complicated technical and scientific developments that it is a matter for special study. But a bare description of the nature of each process will perhaps be of some value.

All ways of multiplying designs for illustration have as their basis one of three methods, all of which can be either *autographic* or *photographic*. That is, the design can be made by the artist himself on the printing surface, or it can be photographically transferred to a sensitised printing surface. And in the latter method the illustration to be reproduced can be not only an original design but a photograph or an illustration already made by one of the autographic methods. Also, nearly all the processes, whether autographic or photographic, can now be printed in colour as well as in monochrome.

First, the design may be drawn direct on to the printing surface and the white parts are cut away to a lower level leaving the black lines or masses in *relief*. The block can therefore be printed with the type in an ordinary press. Secondly, the design can be incised or bitten on a metal plate, usually of copper, which after being inked is wiped clean, leaving the furrows to hold the ink. In this *engraved* method, known as *intaglio*, the pressure has to be strong enough to force the paper, which has to be damped, into the hollows and pull out the ink. The illustration cannot therefore be printed simultaneously with the letterpress. Thirdly, the design may be drawn direct or transferred to the flat *surface* of a specially prepared stone or metal plate. The basis of this process is the antipathy of grease to water, the design being drawn with brush, pen or crayon in a fatty substance to which the ink adheres while the damp stone rejects the ink elsewhere.

AUTOGRAPHIC PROCESSES

(a) RELIEF

The *woodcut* is made with a knife and gouges on the soft or plank side of the wood, the pattern being conceived as contrasted masses of black and white or in thick black outlines on the negative white background of the paper. It is, however, equally possible to integrate the black as a positive part of the pattern and to engrave a design in much thinner white lines, using a graver on a section of hard wood, usually box, cut across the grain. This technique of *wood-engraving* has remained unaltered since the time of Bewick. The number of impressions that can be taken is limited and to-day it is customary to make an electrotype from the wood if a large edition of a book is contemplated. A coloured illustration can be obtained by a series of blocks, one for each colour, which are printed one over another. Linoleum is another material that can be used for relief printing, but owing to its softness the lines in a *linocut* are coarser than those of a woodcut.

(b) ENGRAVED

There are several intaglio processes, the most important of which are line-engraving, etching, drypoint, aquatint, mezzotint and stipple. Two or more of these are frequently combined on one plate. The first three depend for their effect on the use of line ; the last three are essentially tone processes and were commonly so used in the late eighteenth and early nineteenth centuries for the imitation of water-colours, oil-paintings and chalk drawings respectively. Mezzotint and stipple are no longer used in book-illustration. In a *line-engraving* the design is cut into a highly polished copper plate with a sharp pointed burin which is pushed from the palm of the hand in a constant direction, curves being made by turning the plate. The plate rests on a small leather-covered sandbag. This technique accounts for the severe formal quality of the line. After the ink has been worked into the furrows the plate is wiped clean and the paper laid on the plate, which is then passed between the two rollers of a press resembling a household mangle. Owing to the softness of copper the number of impressions is limited.

A *steel-engraving* is made in the same way, but as the metal is so much harder it is possible to cut very fine lines which give great brilliancy. For book-illustration it is now usual to deposit a facing of steel by electrolysis after a copper plate has been engraved. An unlimited number of impressions may then be taken.

In a *drypoint* a steel needle replaces the burin and, held like a pencil, it throws up a burr of metal to one side of the furrow. The burr is not scraped away and gives an added richness to the line. It does not long resist the pressure of printing, and after about thirty impressions the quality is affected.

The *mezzotint* differs from all the other intaglio processes in that the artist works from black to white. The whole plate is roughened with a rocker and if then printed would give a dense black mass. The medium tones are obtained by scraping down the burr in varying degrees until the high lights are reached. These are not merely scraped right down but are polished with a burnisher so that no roughness or burr is left to hold any ink. The essential quality of the process is the rich velvety black which can be obtained in the dark tones and its lovely gleam for the rendering of hair, rich stuffs, weapons and other accessories of portrait painting. It was, therefore, the medium suited above all others for the reproduction of oil-paintings. In the art of landscape it was used for two notable series of plates—Turner's *Liber Studiorum* and Constable's landscapes engraved by David Lucas.

There remain two intaglio processes in which the plate is not cut by hand but bitten by acid. In *etching* the plate is first coated with a thin "ground" of wax and asphaltum which is blackened over a lighted taper. The design is cut through the ground, laying bare but not cutting the copper. The plate is then etched in a bath of acid until the parts which are to print lightest are eaten away. These are varnished or "stopped", and the process is repeated until the darkest parts have been bitten to the requisite depth. An etching is far freer in style than a line-engraving, as there is no resistance to the needle. The effect of a pencil or chalk drawing can be successfully imitated by *soft ground etching* in which the design is drawn in pencil or chalk on a thin piece of paper which is stretched over the "soft-ground"—a mixture of ordinary ground and tallow. When the paper is lifted the ground adheres where there has been pressure from the pencil, the grain of which is reproduced when the plate is bitten.

As in etching the plate of an *aquatint* is bitten by acid. But the aim is to reproduce tone and not line, and the essence of the process is the rendering of flat tints of varying depths by means of a porous ground through whose grains the acid can bite. The grounds can be laid either with a dust of powdered resin or asphaltum, or with a solution of shellac in alcohol. In the former method the dust is put into a box where it is blown into a cloud which settles evenly on the plate, the back of which is then heated so that the ground adheres. In the second method the plate is flooded with the solution which, as it dries, crackles all over the plate. The technique of stopping the lightest tints is effected as in etching. Colour was commonly added to aquatints, either being printed off the plate or more often being added by hand in imitation of water-colours, for the reproduction of which aquatint was frequently used.

(c) SURFACE

The story goes that Senefelder accidentally discovered *lithography* by writing down a bill for the washerwoman—no paper being at hand —in an ink of wax, soap and lampblack on a polished stone which he used as a practising-ground for the looking-glass writing necessary for copperplate engraving. He suddenly thought of damping the stone, which would then retain the moisture where his grease-writing had not touched it and would reject the greasy printing-ink to be next applied and to be retained only by the greasy chalk. Satisfactory impressions were taken by passing the paper and stone beneath a wooden scraper. From such simple beginnings sprang the art of lithography, which in its essentials remains unaltered to-day when practised in the studio. A large variety of textures are possible in lithography, as the stone or plate can be grained rough to give a print resembling a chalk drawing, or it can be polished for use with a pen, brush, knife or even an air-brush. The design can also be drawn on a special coated paper from which it is transferred on to the stone. This enables the artist to work in the open and the image is drawn in the ordinary way and not in reverse. Lithography is an admirable process for colour-work. Many tones of the same colour can be used in one subject; almost any kind of paper can be used; and outlines and accents of drawing can be rendered in a manner beyond the range of photographic colour process.

Senefelder had himself experimented with two or more plates to produce a few neutral tones, and this technique was notably developed from about 1825 onwards under the name of *lithotint*. The different graduated tones were obtained with a liquid solution of chalk which was brushed on to the stone. Where required these were scraped down to give white high lights.

To-day the greater part of lithographic printing is by the *offset* process, so called because an extra cylinder thinly covered with a rubber blanket receives the print from the stone or plate and passes it to the paper. The image need not, therefore, be drawn in reverse. Nearly all commercial lithographic illustration is now reproduced by the offset method from zinc plates which can be bent round the cylinders of rotary printing machines.

PHOTOGRAPHIC PROCESSES

(a) RELIEF

The earliest and simplest of the photographic processes is the *line-block*, which can be made from any subject that has no gradation of tone. A photographic negative, made from the drawing, is printed in positive on a sensitised emulsion on a sheet of zinc. The light passes through the transparent parts of the negative which correspond to the lines of the drawing, and hardens the emulsion on those parts only. The rest of the emulsion is washed away and the remaining parts forming the design are dusted with powdered resin which forms an acid-resist. The plate is then etched in a bath of acid which eats away the background to a depth which will not be touched by the ink roller or the paper in the printing machine. The zinc plate (which gave the line-block its first name of *zincograph*) is then mounted type-high on a wooden block and printed with the text on the same paper.

For the reproduction of a continuous or graduated tone the method known as *half-tone* is most used because it is the cheapest. The original, which can be a photograph or a drawing, is in this instance photographed through a glass screen covered with lines crossing at right angles. This splits up the original into a mass of tiny dots of varying size. Where the tone is dark the dots are large and nearly continuous, in the light parts they are smaller and widely spaced. The negative is printed on to a sensitised copper plate and etched in the same way as for a line-block, but if the contrasts of tone are to be accurate, the plate has to be re-etched in stages with the appropriate stopping-out as for an ordinary etching. The dots of copper then become the printing-surface and if a really faithful reproduction is to be obtained a coated "art" paper is necessary. This paper tears easily, dazzles the eyes, and is ruined beyond repair by damp.

The colour version of half-tone was introduced as the *three-colour process*, being based on the Newtonian principle that all colours can be obtained by a mixture of the three primaries, red, yellow and blue in varying amounts. A German named Jakob Le Blon made successful experiments in this direction as early as 1711, and published a book in London called *Coloritto* in 1772, which has colour plates built up by three impressions taken from engraved plates. Here the appropriate overlapping of colours had to be calculated by the eye, but in modern three-colour work the original is split up by being photographed three times, exposure being made through a glass colour filter which allows only one primary colour to pass into the camera. From each of the three negatives a half-tone block is made by means of a screen as in the manner of monochrome half-tone. It was soon discovered that for the strong and deeper tones a fourth block printed in black was desirable; and virtually all process work in colour to-day is in four colours. Although the colour analysis is theoretically made by the camera, a good deal of re-etching has to be done by hand. The cost of the blocks is high and there is the same compulsion to use a coated paper.

(b) ENGRAVING

The combination of photography and engraving known as *photo-gravure* preceded by a few years the line-block in the illustration of books. Etchings were, at that time, a popular form of graphic art and the new process was well suited to their reproduction although it was slow and costly. The subject was photographed on to a flat copper plate which was then dusted as for an aquatint with powder which formed an almost invisible screen of dots round which the acid could bite. To-day the ruled screen of crossed lines applied photographically has replaced the dust screen and printing is done from a copper cylinder. As in all engraved processes, a rich deep tone is obtained and the ordinary text paper can be used. Unless the letterpress is separately printed any accompanying text must also be photographed on to the cylinder. The process is therefore popular for books consisting mainly of plates taken from photographs.

(c) SURFACE

When the image is photographed instead of being drawn by the artist on the zinc plate used in offset-lithography the process is called *photo-litho-offset*. In monochrome, it gives a good facsimile of line-drawings or, with the additional use of the half-tone screen, subjects with tonal qualities; and although it lacks the brilliance and crispness of half-tone it can be used on a paper with a natural surface. Even a line-engraving or etching can be reproduced without undue loss of the finest detail, so sensitive is the pressure of the rubber blanket of the offset process. It can also be used for reproductive colour work on the four-colour principle provided that the subject is restricted in its range of tones and has a thin pastel or water-colour quality. A number of additional printings will still be required to obtain sufficient strength of colour in facsimile reproductions of many drawings in colour.

Of all reproductive processes based on photography, *collotype* is the most attractive. Like lithography it is printed from a flat surface, but as this consists of sensitised gelatine, only comparatively few impressions can be taken before the surface becomes worn. It is, therefore, only suitable for relatively small editions up to 1,500 copies. The gelatine is laid on a thick piece of plate glass, and after it has received the image it hardens in proportion to the amount of light passing through the various parts of the negative, which retain more or less moisture according to the tonal values of the original. This variation of moisture produces a graduated feed of ink which gives a wonderfully even gradation of tone without any breaking up of the image into dots. It is, above all, suitable for the reproduction of drawings and paintings. When used as a colour process it has all the advantages of the four-colour process and none of the drawbacks. It has in recent years been successfully combined with stencil work and lithography.

SHORT BIBLIOGRAPHY

THE BROTHERS DALZIEL. *A record of fifty years' work . . . 1840-1890.* 1901.

HARDIE, M. *English coloured books.* 1906.

WHITE, G. *English illustration : the sixties.* 3rd impression. 1906.

BURCH, R. M. *Colour printing and colour printers.* 1910.

JACKSON, H. *The eighteen-nineties.* 1913, *etc.* Reprinted in Pelican Books. 1939.

British book illustrations yesterday and to-day. Studio special number (Winter, 1923-24).

PRINT SOCIETY. *How to distinguish prints.* . . . Edited by H. Hubbard. 1926.

REID, F. *Illustrators of the 'sixties.* 1928.

SYMONS, A. J. A. *An unacknowledged movement in fine printing (the 1890's).* Article in *The Fleuron*, no. vii. 1930.

LONDON: BRITISH MUSEUM. *A guide to the processes and schools of engraving.* 1933.

CURWEN, H. *Processes of graphic reproduction in printing.* 1934.

BALSTON, T. *English book illustrations, 1800-1900.* Chapter in *New paths in book collecting.* . . . Edited by J. Carter. 1934.

THORPE, J. *English illustration: the 'nineties.* 1935.

GRAY, B. *The English print.* 1937.

LEWIS, C. T. C. *The story of picture printing in England during the nineteenth century.* n.d.

INDEX OF ILLUSTRATORS

J. RUSKIN. Foreground leafage. From *Modern Painters*, vol. iii, 1856.
(Steel-engraving by J. C. Armytage.)

What time the king-fisher sits perched below,
Where, silver-bright, the water-lilies blow:—
A Wake—the booths whitening the village-green,
Where Punch and Scaramouch aloft are seen;
Sign beyond sign in close array unfurled,
Picturing at large the wonders of the world;

J. M. W. TURNER.   " A Wake—the booths whitening the village green."
From *Human Life* in S. Rogers, *Poems*, 1834. (Steel-engraving by E. Goodall.)

I.

'Twas Autumn; thro' Provence had ceased
The vintage, and the vintage-feast.
The sun had set behind the hill,
The moon was up, and all was still,
And from the Convent's neighbouring tower
The clock had tolled the midnight-hour,
When Jacqueline came forth alone,
Her kerchief o'er her tresses thrown;
A guilty thing and full of fears,
Yet ah, how lovely in her tears!

T. STOTHARD. 'The Grape-harvest.'
From *Jacqueline* in S. Rogers, *Poems*, 1834. (Steel-engraving by W. Findon.)

4

G. CRUIKSHANK. Fagin in the condemned cell. From C. Dickens, *Oliver Twist*, 1838. (Etching.)

G. CRUIKSHANK. All a-growing. From *The Comic Almanack*, May, 1838. (Etching.)

6

J. MARTIN. Psalm cxxxvii, " By the waters of Babylon we sat down and wept."
From *Illustrations of the Bible*, 1831-5. (Mezzotint.)

S. PALMER.   Opening the fold ; or Early morning.
From *An English version of the Eclogues of Virgil.*   1883.   (Etching.)

F. 45.

London, Published December 2nd 1861 by Day & Son, Lith to the Queen.

J. McN. WHISTLER. A river scene. From Passages from modern English poets,

T. ROWLANDSON. The Honey-Moon—"When the old Fool has drunk his wine, and gone to rest—I will be thine." From *The English Dance of Death* (by W. Combe). 2 vols. 1815-16. (Aquatint).

P. REINAGLE. The Night-Blowing Cereus, or, Cactus Grandiflorus.
From R. J. Thornton, *The Temple of Flora*. 1797-1807. (Aquatint and
mezzotint by Dunkarton.)

J. LEECH. *Juvenile :* I say, Harriet, do us a favour ?
Pretty Cousin : Well, what is it ?
Juvenile : Give us a lock of your hair to take back to. school.
From *The Rising Generation. A series of twelve drawings on stone. From his
original designs in the gallery of Mr. Punch.* 1848. (Hand coloured lithograph.)

R. CALDECOTT. The Parish Priest. From Mrs. Comyns Carr, *North Italian Folk*. 1878. (Hand coloured wood-engraving.)

R. DOYLE. (a) Flirting, (b) The Fairy Queen's Messenger. From *In Fairyland . . . with a poem by W. Allingham.* 1870. (Wood-engraving by E. Evans.)

SIR W. NICHOLSON. Hammersmith. From *London Types*. Quator-
zains by *W. E. Henley*. 1898. (Lithograph from original coloured woodcut.)

L. PISSARRO.   Frontispiece from S. T. Coleridge, *Christabel*, Kubla Khan,
etc.   Eragny Press, 1904.   (Wood-engraving.)

But whilst he strutted through the street,
  With looks both vain and pert,
A sweep-boy pass'd, whom not to meet,
  He slipp'd—into the dirt.
The sooty lad, whose heart was kind,
  To help him quickly ran,
And grasp'd his arm, with—" Never mind,
  You're up, my little man."

Sweep wiped his clothes with labour vain,
  And begg'd him not to cry;
And when he'd blacken'd every stain,
  Said, " Little sir, good-bye."
Poor George, almost as dark as sweep,
  And smear'd in dress and face,
Bemoans with sobs, both loud and deep,
  His well-deserved disgrace.

KATE GREENAWAY. George and the Chimney-Sweep. From Jane
and Ann Taylor, *Little Ann and other poems.* 1883. (Colour wood-engraving
by E. Evans.)